APOSTOLIC LETTER

TERTIO MILLENNIO ADVENIENTE

OF HIS HOLINESS

POPE JOHN PAUL II

TO THE BISHOPS, CLERGY

AND LAY FAITHFUL

ON PREPARATION

FOR THE JUBILEE OF THE YEAR 2000

LIBRERIA EDITRICE VATICANA

VATICAN CITY

CONTENTS

To the Bishops,
Priests and Deacons,
Men and Women Religious,
and all the Lay Faithful

1.   A S THE THIRD MILLENNIUM of the new era draws near, our thoughts turn spontaneously to the words of the Apostle Paul: "When the fullness of time had come, God sent forth his Son, born of woman" (*Gal* 4:4). *The fullness of time coincides with the mystery of the Incarnation of the Word,* of the Son who is of one being with the Father, and with the mystery of the Redemption of the world. In this passage, Saint Paul emphasizes that the Son of God was born of woman, born under the Law, and came into the world in order to redeem all who were under the Law, so that they might receive adoption as sons and daughters. And he adds: "Because you are sons, God has sent the Spirit of his Son into our hearts, crying 'Abba! Father!'" His conclusion is truly comforting: "So through God you are no longer a slave but a son, and if a son then an heir" (*Gal* 4:6-7).

Paul's presentation of the mystery of the Incarnation contains *the revelation of the mystery of the Trinity and the continuation of the Son's mission in the mission of the Holy Spirit.* The Incarnation of the Son of God, his conception and birth, is the prerequisite for the sending of the Holy Spirit. This text of Saint Paul *thus allows the fullness of the mystery of the Redemptive Incarnation to shine forth.*

I

"JESUS CHRIST IS THE SAME YESTERDAY AND TODAY"
(*Heb* 13:8)

2.   In his Gospel Luke has handed down to us a *concise narrative of the circumstances of Jesus' birth:* "In those days a decree went out from Caesar Augustus that all the world should be enrolled ... And all went to be enrolled, each to his own city. And Joseph also went up from Galilee, from the city of Nazareth, to Judea, to the city of David, which is called Bethlehem, because he was of the house and lineage of David, to be enrolled with Mary, his betrothed, who was with child. And while they were there, the time came for her to be delivered. And she gave birth to her first-born son and wrapped him in swaddling cloths, and laid him in a manger, because there was no place for them in the inn" (2:1, 3-7).

Thus was fulfilled what the Angel Gabriel foretold at the Annunciation, when he spoke to the Virgin of Nazareth in these words: "Hail, full of grace, the Lord is with you" (1:28). Mary was troubled by these words, and so the divine messenger quickly added: "Do not be afraid, Mary, for you have found favour with God. And behold, you will conceive in your womb and bear a son, and you shall call his name Jesus. He will be great and will be called the Son of the Most High ... The Holy Spirit will come upon you and the power of the Most High will overshadow you; therefore the child to be born will be called holy, the Son of God" (1:32-33, 35). Mary's reply to the angel was unhesitating: "Behold, I am the handmaid of the Lord; let it be to me according to your word" (1:38). Never in human history did so much depend, as it did then, upon the consent of one human creature.[1]

3.   John, in the Prologue of his Gospel, captures in one phrase all the depth of the mystery of the Incarnation. He writes: *"And the Word became flesh and dwelt among us,* full of grace and truth; we have beheld his glory, glory as of the only Son from the Father" (1:14). For John, the Incarnation of the Eternal Word, of one being with the Father, took place in the conception and birth of Jesus. The Evangelist speaks of the Word who in the beginning was with God, and through whom everything which exists was made; the Word in whom was life, the life which was the light of men (cf. 1:1-4). Of the Only-Begotten Son, God from God, the Apostle Paul writes that he is *"the first-born of all creation"* (*Col* 1:15). God created the world through the Word. The Word is Eternal Wisdom; the Thought and Substantial Image of God; "He reflects the glory of God and bears

---

[1] Cf. Saint Bernard, *In Laudibus Virginis Matris, Homilia IV,* 8, *Opera omnia,* Edit. Cisterc. (1966), 53.

6

the very stamp of his nature" (*Heb* 1:3). Eternally begotten and eternally loved by the Father, as God from God and Light from Light, he is the principle and archetype of everything created by God in time.

The fact that in the fullness of time the Eternal Word took on the condition of a creature gives a unique *cosmic value* to the event which took place in Bethlehem two thousand years ago. *Thanks to the Word, the world of creatures appears as a "cosmos",* an ordered universe. And it is the same Word who, *by taking flesh, renews the cosmic order of creation.* The Letter to the Ephesians speaks of the purpose which God had set forth in Christ, "as a plan for the fullness of time, *to unite all things in him,* things in heaven and things on earth" (1:9-10).

4.　　Christ, the Redeemer of the world, *is the one Mediator between God and men,* and there is no other name under heaven by which we can be saved (cf. *Acts* 4:12). As we read in the Letter to the Ephesians: "in him, we have redemption through his blood, the forgiveness of our trespasses, according to the richness of his grace, which he has lavished upon us. For he has made known to us in all wisdom and insight ... his purpose which he set forth in Christ as a plan for the fullness of time, to unite all things in him, things in heaven and things on earth" (1:7-10). Christ, the Son who is of one being with the Father, is therefore the one who *reveals God's plan for all creation, and for man in particular.* In the memorable phrase

7

of the Second Vatican Council, Christ *"fully reveals man to man himself and makes his supreme calling clear"*.[2] He shows us this calling by revealing the mystery of the Father and his love. As the image of the invisible God, Christ is the perfect man who has restored to the children of Adam the divine likeness which had been deformed by sin. In his human nature, free from all sin and assumed into the divine Person of the Word, the nature shared by all human beings is raised to a sublime dignity: "By his incarnation the Son of God *united himself in some sense with every man.* He laboured with human hands, thought with a human mind, acted with a human will, and loved with a human heart. Born of Mary the Virgin he truly became one of us and, sin apart, was like us in every way".[3]

5.   This "becoming one of us" on the part of the Son of God took place in the greatest humility, so it is no wonder that secular historians, caught up by more stirring events and by famous personages, first made only passing, albeit significant, references to him. Such references to Christ are found for example in *The Antiquities of the Jews,* a work compiled in Rome between the years 93 and 94 by the historian Flavius Josephus,[4] and especially in the *Annals* of Tacitus, written be-

---

[2] Pastoral Constitution on the Church in the Modern World *Gaudium et Spes,* 22.

[3] *Ibid.*

[4] Cf. *Ant. Iud.* 20:200, and the well-known and much-discussed passage in 18:63-64.

tween the years 115 and 120, where, reporting the burning of Rome in the year 64, falsely attributed by Nero to the Christians, the historian makes an explicit reference to Christ "executed by order of the procurator Pontius Pilate during the reign of Tiberius".[5] Suetonius too, in his biography of the Emperor Claudius, written around 121, informs us that the Jews were expelled from Rome because "under the instigation of a certain Chrestus they stirred up frequent riots".[6] This passage is generally interpreted as referring to Jesus Christ, who had become a source of contention within Jewish circles in Rome. Also of importance as proof of the rapid spread of Christianity is the testimony of Pliny the Younger, the Governor of Bithynia, who reported to the Emperor Trajan, between the years 111 and 113, that a large number of people was accustomed to gather "on a designated day, before dawn, to sing in alternating choirs a hymn to Christ as to a God".[7]

But the great event which non-Christian historians merely mention in passing takes on its full significance in the writings of the New Testament. These writings, although documents of faith, are no less reliable as historical testimonies, if we consider their references as a whole. Christ, true God and true man, the Lord of the cosmos, is also the Lord of history, of which he is "the Alpha and the Omega" (*Rev* 1:8; 21:6), "the beginning and the

[5] *Annales* 15:44. 3.
[6] *Vita Claudii*, 25:4.
[7] *Epist.* 10:96.

end" (*Rev* 21:6). In him the Father has spoken the definitive word about mankind and its history. This is expressed in a concise and powerful way by the Letter to the Hebrews: "In many and various ways God spoke of old to our fathers by the prophets; *but in these last days he has spoken to us by a Son*" (1:1-2).

6.   Jesus was born of the Chosen People, in fulfilment of the promise made to Abraham and constantly recalled by the Prophets. The latter spoke in God's name and in his place. The economy of the Old Testament, in fact, was essentially ordered to preparing and proclaiming the coming of Christ, the Redeemer of the universe, and of his Messianic Kingdom. The books of the Old Covenant are thus a permanent witness to a careful divine pedagogy.[8] *In Christ* this pedagogy achieves its purpose: Jesus does not in fact merely speak "in the name of God" like the Prophets, but he is God himself speaking in his Eternal Word made flesh. Here we touch upon *the essential point by which Christianity differs from all the other religions,* by which *man's search for God* has been expressed from earliest times. Christianity has its starting-point in the Incarnation of the Word. Here, it is not simply a case of man seeking God, but of God who comes in Person to speak to man of himself and to show him the path by which he may be reached. This is what is proclaimed in the

---

[8] Cf. SECOND VATICAN ECUMENICAL COUNCIL, Dogmatic Constitution on Divine Revelation *Dei Verbum,* 15.

Prologue of John's Gospel: "No one has ever seen God; the only Son, who is in the bosom of the Father, he has made him known" (1:18). *The Incarnate Word is thus the fulfilment of the yearning present in all the religions of mankind:* this fulfilment is brought about by God himself and transcends all human expectations. It is the mystery of grace.

In Christ, religion is no longer a "blind search for God" (cf. *Acts* 17:27) but the *response of faith* to God who reveals himself. It is a response in which man speaks to God as his Creator and Father, a response made possible by that one Man who is also the consubstantial Word in whom God speaks to each individual person and by whom each individual person is enabled to respond to God. What is more, in this Man all creation responds to God. Jesus Christ is the new beginning of everything. In him all things come into their own; they are taken up and given back to the Creator from whom they first came. *Christ is thus the fulfilment of the yearning of all the world's religions and, as such, he is their sole and definitive completion.* Just as God in Christ speaks to humanity of himself, so in Christ all humanity and the whole of creation speaks of itself to God—indeed, it gives itself to God. Everything thus returns to its origin. *Jesus Christ is the recapitulation of everything* (cf. *Eph* 1:10) and at the same time the fulfilment of all things in God: a fulfilment which is the glory of God. The religion founded upon Jesus Christ is a *religion of glory;* it is a newness of life for the praise of the glory of

God (cf. *Eph* 1:12). All creation is in reality a manifestation of his glory. In particular, man *(vivens homo)* is the epiphany of God's glory, man who is called to live by the fullness of life in God.

7.   *In Jesus Christ* God not only speaks to man but also *seeks him out.* The Incarnation of the Son of God attests that God goes in search of man. Jesus speaks of this search as the finding of a lost sheep (cf. *Lk* 15:1-7). It is a search which *begins in the heart of God* and culminates in the Incarnation of the Word. If God goes in search of man, created in his own image and likeness, he does so because he loves him eternally in the Word, and wishes to raise him in Christ to the dignity of an adoptive son. God therefore goes in search of man who *is his special possession* in a way unlike any other creature. Man is God's possession by virtue of a choice made in love: God seeks man out, moved by his fatherly heart.

Why does God seek man out? Because man has turned away from him, hiding himself as Adam did among the trees of the Garden of Eden (cf. *Gen* 3:8-10). *Man allowed himself to be led astray* by the enemy of God (cf. *Gen* 3:13). Satan deceived man, persuading him that he too was a god, that he, like God, was capable of knowing good and evil, ruling the world according to his own will without having to take into account the divine will (cf. *Gen* 3:5). Going in search of man through his Son, God wishes to persuade man to abandon the paths of evil which lead him farther and farther afield. "Making him abandon" those

12

paths means making man understand that he is taking the wrong path; it means *overcoming the evil* which is everywhere found in human history. *Overcoming evil: this is the meaning of the Redemption.* This is brought about in the sacrifice of Christ, by which man redeems the debt of sin and is reconciled to God. The Son of God became man, taking a body and soul in the womb of the Virgin, precisely for this reason: to become the perfect redeeming sacrifice. The religion of the Incarnation is the *religion* of the world's *Redemption* through the sacrifice of Christ, wherein lies victory over evil, over sin and over death itself. Accepting death on the Cross, Christ at the same time reveals and gives life, because he rises again and death no longer has power over him.

8.   The religion which originates in the mystery of the Redemptive Incarnation, is the religion of *"dwelling in the heart of God"*, of sharing in God's very life. Saint Paul speaks of this in the passage already quoted: "God has sent the Spirit of his Son into our hearts, crying, 'Abba! Father!' " (*Gal* 4:6). Man cries out like Christ himself, who turned to God "with loud cries and tears" (*Heb* 5:7), especially in Gethsemane and on the Cross: man cries out to God just as Christ cried out to him, and thus he bears witness that he shares in Christ's sonship through the power of the Holy Spirit. The Holy Spirit, whom the Father has sent in the name of the Son, enables man to share in the inmost life of God. He also enables man *to be a son, in the likeness of Christ,* and an heir of all

that belongs to the Son (cf. *Gal* 4:7). In this consists the religion of "dwelling in the inmost life of God", which begins with the Incarnation of the Son of God. The Holy Spirit, who searches the depths of God (cf. *1 Cor* 2:10), leads us, all mankind, into these depths by virtue of the sacrifice of Christ.

II

THE JUBILEE OF THE YEAR 2000

9.   Speaking of the birth of the Son of God, Saint Paul places this event in the "fullness of time" (cf. *Gal* 4:4). *Time is indeed fulfilled by the very fact that God, in the Incarnation, came down into human history.* Eternity entered into time: what "fulfilment" could be greater than this? What other "fulfilment" would be possible? Some have thought in terms of certain *mysterious cosmic cycles* in which the history of the universe, and of mankind in particular, would constantly repeat itself. True, man rises from the earth and returns to it (cf. *Gen* 3:19): this is an immediately evident fact. Yet in man there is an irrepressible longing to live forever. How are we to imagine a life beyond death? Some have considered various forms of *reincarnation:* depending on one's previous life, one would receive a new life in either a higher or lower form, until full purification is attained. This belief, deeply rooted in some Eastern religions, itself indicates that man rebels against the finality of death. He is convinced that his nature is essentially spiritual and immortal.

Christian revelation excludes reincarnation, and speaks of a fulfilment which man is called to achieve in the course of a single earthly existence.

Man achieves this fulfilment of his destiny through the sincere gift of self, a gift which is made possible only through his encounter with God. It is in God that man finds full self-realization: *this is the truth revealed by Christ.* Man fulfils himself in God, who comes to meet him through his Eternal Son. Thanks to God's coming on earth, human time, which began at Creation, has reached its fullness. "The fullness of time" is in fact eternity, indeed, it is *the One who is eternal,* God himself. Thus, to enter into "the fullness of time" means to reach the end of time and to transcend its limits, in order to find time's fulfilment in the eternity of God.

10.   *In Christianity time has a fundamental importance.* Within the dimension of time the world was created; within it the history of salvation unfolds, finding its culmination in the "fullness of time" of the Incarnation, and its goal in the glorious return of the Son of God at the end of time. *In Jesus Christ, the Word made flesh, time becomes a dimension of God,* who is himself eternal. With the coming of Christ there begin "the last days" (cf. *Heb* 1:2), the "last hour" (cf. *1 Jn* 2:18), and the time of the Church, which will last until the Parousia.

From this relationship of God with time there arises *the duty to sanctify time.* This is done, for example, when individual times, days or weeks, are dedicated to God, as once happened in the religion of the Old Covenant, and as happens still, though in a new way, in Christianity. In the liturgy of the Easter Vigil the celebrant, as he blesses

the candle which symbolizes the Risen Christ, proclaims: "Christ yesterday and today, the beginning
and the end, Alpha and Omega, all time belongs
to him, and all the ages, to him be glory and
power through every age for ever". He says these
words as he inscribes on the candle the numerals
of the current year. The meaning of this rite is
clear: it emphasizes the fact that *Christ is the Lord
of time;* he is its beginning and its end; every year,
every day and every moment are embraced by his
Incarnation and Resurrection, and thus become
part of the "fullness of time". For this reason, the
Church too lives and celebrates the liturgy in the
span of a year. *The solar year is thus permeated by
the liturgical year,* which in a certain way repro-
duces the whole mystery of the Incarnation and
Redemption, beginning from the First Sunday of
Advent and ending on the Solemnity of Christ the
King, Lord of the Universe and Lord of History.
Every Sunday commemorates the day of the
Lord's Resurrection.

11.   Against this background, we can understand *the custom of Jubilees,* which began in the
Old Testament and continues in the history of the
Church. Jesus of Nazareth, going back one day to
the *synagogue of his home town,* stood up to read
(cf. *Lk* 4:16-30). Taking the book of the Prophet
Isaiah, he read this passage: "The Spirit of the
Lord God is upon me, because the Lord has
anointed me to bring good tidings to the afflicted;
he has sent me to bind up the brokenhearted, to
proclaim liberty to the captives, and the opening

17

of the prison to those who are bound; *to proclaim the year of the Lord's favour*" (61:1-2).

The Prophet was speaking of the Messiah. "Today", Jesus added, "this scripture has been fulfilled in your hearing" (*Lk* 4:21), thus indicating that he himself was the Messiah foretold by the Prophet, and that the long-expected "time" was beginning in him. The day of salvation had come, the "fullness of time". *All Jubilees point to this "time" and refer to the Messianic mission of Christ,* who came as the one "anointed" by the Holy Spirit, the one "sent by the Father". It is he who proclaims the good news to the poor. It is he who brings liberty to those deprived of it, who frees the oppressed and gives back sight to the blind (cf. *Mt* 11:4-5; *Lk* 7:22). In this way he ushers in "a year of the Lord's favour", which he proclaims not only with his words but above all by his actions. The Jubilee, "a year of the Lord's favour", characterizes all the activity of Jesus; it is not merely the recurrence of an anniversary in time.

12.   *The words and deeds of Jesus thus represent the fulfilment of the whole tradition of Jubilees* in the Old Testament. We know that the Jubilee was *a time dedicated in a special way to God.* It fell every seventh year, according to the Law of Moses: this was the "sabbatical year", during which the earth was left fallow and slaves were set free. The duty to free slaves was regulated by detailed prescriptions contained in the Books of Exodus (23:10-11), Leviticus (25:1-28) and Deuteronomy

18

(15:1-6). In other words, these prescriptions are found in practically the whole of biblical legislation, which is thus marked by this very specific characteristic. In the sabbatical year, in addition to the freeing of slaves the Law also provided for the cancellation of all debts in accordance with precise regulations. And all this was to be done in honour of God. What was true for the sabbatical year was also true for the *jubilee* year, which fell every fifty years. In the jubilee year, however, the customs of the sabbatical year were broadened and celebrated with even greater solemnity. As we read in Leviticus: "You shall hallow the fiftieth year, and proclaim liberty throughout the land to all its inhabitants; it shall be a jubilee for you, when each of you shall return to his property and each of you shall return to his family" (25:10). One of the most significant consequences of the jubilee year was the general *"emancipation" of all the dwellers on the land in need of being freed.* On this occasion every Israelite regained possession of his ancestral land, if he happened to have sold it or lost it by falling into slavery. He could never be completely deprived of the land, because it belonged to God; nor could the Israelites remain for ever in a state of slavery, since God had "redeemed" them for himself as his exclusive possession by freeing them from slavery in Egypt.

13. The prescriptions for the jubilee year largely remained ideals—more a hope than an actual fact. They thus became a *prophetia futuri* insofar as they foretold the freedom which would be won by the

19

coming Messiah. Even so, on the basis of the juridical norms contained in these prescriptions a kind of *social doctrine* began to emerge, which would then more clearly develop beginning with the New Testament. *The jubilee year was meant to restore equality among all the children of Israel,* offering new possibilities to families which had lost their property and even their personal freedom. On the other hand, the jubilee year was a reminder to the rich that a time would come when their Israelite slaves would once again become their equals and would be able to reclaim their rights. At the times prescribed by Law, a jubilee year had to be proclaimed, to assist those in need. This was required by just government. *Justice, according to the Law of Israel, consisted above all in the protection of the weak,* and a king was supposed to be outstanding in this regard, as the Psalmist says: "He delivers the needy when he calls, the poor and him who has no helper. He has pity on the weak and the needy, and saves the lives of the needy" (*Ps* 72:12-13). *The foundations of this tradition were strictly theological,* linked first of all with the theology of Creation and with that of Divine Providence. It was a common conviction, in fact, that *to God alone, as Creator, belonged the "dominium altum"*—lordship over all Creation and over the earth in particular (cf. *Lev* 25:23). If in his Providence God had given the earth to humanity, that meant that he had given it to everyone. Therefore *the riches of Creation were to be considered as a common good of the whole of humanity.* Those who possessed these goods as personal property were really only stewards, ministers charged with working in the name of God, who remains the sole owner in the full sense, since it is God's will that created goods should serve everyone in a just way. *The jubilee year was meant to restore this social justice.* The social doctrine of the Church, which has always been a part of Church teaching and which has developed greatly in the last century, particularly after the Encyclical *Rerum Novarum,* is rooted in the tradition of the jubilee year.

14.   What needs to be emphasized, however, is what Isaiah expresses in the words *"to proclaim the year of the Lord's favour".* For the Church, the Jubilee is precisely this "year of the Lord's favour", a year of the remission of sins and of the punishments due to them, a year of reconciliation between disputing parties, a year of manifold conversions and of sacramental and extra-sacramental penance. The tradition of jubilee years involves the *granting* of indulgences on a larger scale than at other times. Together with Jubilees recalling the mystery of the Incarnation, at intervals of a hundred, fifty and twenty-five years, there are also Jubilees which commemorate the event of the Redemption: the Cross of Christ, his death on Golgotha and the Resurrection. On these occasions, the Church proclaims "a year of the Lord's favour", and she tries to ensure that all the faithful can benefit from this grace. *That is why Jubilees are celebrated not only "in Urbe" but also "extra Urbem":* traditionally the latter took place the year after the celebration "in Urbe".

15.   *In the lives of individuals, Jubilees* are usually connected with the date of birth; but other anniversaries are also celebrated, such as those of Baptism, Confirmation, First Communion, Priestly or Episcopal Ordination, and the Sacrament of Marriage. Some of these anniversaries have parallels in the secular world, but Christians always give them a religious character. In fact, in the Christian view, every Jubilee—the twenty-fifth of Marriage or Priesthood, known as "silver", the fiftieth, known as "golden", or the sixtieth, known as "diamond"—is a *particular year of favour* for the individual who has received one or other of the Sacraments. What we have said about individuals with regard to jubilees can also be applied to *communities or institutions.* Thus we celebrate the centenary or the millennium of the foundation of a town or city. In the Church, we celebrate the jubilees of parishes and dioceses. All these personal and community Jubilees have an important and significant role in the lives of individuals and communities.

In view of this, *the two thousand years which have passed since the Birth of Christ* (prescinding from the question of its precise chronology) *represent an extraordinarily great Jubilee,* not only for Christians but indirectly for the whole of humanity, given the prominent role played by Christianity during these two millennia. It is significant that the calculation of the passing years begins almost everywhere with the year of Christ's coming into the world, which is thus *the centre* of the calendar most widely used today. Is this not another sign of the unparalleled effect of the Birth of Jesus of Nazareth on the history of mankind?

16. *The term "Jubilee" speaks of joy;* not just an inner joy but a jubilation which is manifested outwardly, for the coming of God is also an outward, visible, audible and tangible event, as Saint John makes clear (cf. *1 Jn* 1:1). It is thus appropriate that every sign of joy at this coming should have its own outward expression. This will demonstrate that *the Church rejoices in salvation.* She invites everyone to rejoice, and she tries to create conditions to ensure that the power of salvation may be shared by all. Hence the Year 2000 will be celebrated as the Great Jubilee.

With regard to its *content, this Great Jubilee* will be, in a certain sense, like any other. But at the same time it will be different, greater than any other. For the Church respects the measurements of time: hours, days, years, centuries. She thus goes forward with every individual, helping everyone to realize how *each of these measurements of time is imbued with the presence of God* and with his saving activity. In this spirit the Church rejoices, gives thanks and asks forgiveness, presenting her petitions to the Lord of history and of human consciences.

Among the most fervent petitions which the Church makes to the Lord during this important time, as the eve of the new millennium approaches, is that unity among all Christians of the various confessions will increase until they reach full communion. I pray that the Jubilee will be a promising opportunity for fruitful cooperation in the many areas which unite us; these are unquestionably more numerous than those which divide us. It would thus be quite helpful if, with due respect for the programmes of the individual Churches and Communities, ecumenical agreements could be reached with regard to the preparation and celebration of the Jubilee. In this way the Jubilee will bear witness even more forcefully before the world that the disciples of Christ are fully resolved to reach full unity as soon as possible in the certainty that "nothing is impossible with God".

III

PREPARATION
FOR THE GREAT JUBILEE

17.   *In the Church's history every jubilee is prepared for by Divine Providence.* This is true also of the Great Jubilee of the Year 2000. With this conviction, we look today with a sense of gratitude and yet with a sense of responsibility at all that has happened in human history since the Birth of Christ, particularly the events which have occurred between the years 1000 and 2000. But in a very particular way, we look with the eyes of faith to our own century, searching out whatever bears witness not only to man's history but also to God's intervention in human affairs.

18.   From this point of view we can affirm that *the Second Vatican Council was a providential event, whereby the Church began the more immediate preparation* for the Jubilee of the Second Millennium. It was a Council similar to earlier ones, yet very different; it was a Council *focused on the mystery of Christ and his Church and at the same time open to the world.* This openness was an evangelical response to recent changes in the world, including the profoundly disturbing experiences of the Twentieth Century, a century scarred by the First

and Second World Wars, by the experience of concentration camps and by horrendous massacres. All these events demonstrate most vividly that the world needs purification; it needs to be converted.

The Second Vatican Council is often considered as the beginning of a new era in the life of the Church. This is true, but at the same time it is difficult to overlook the fact that *the Council drew much from the experiences and reflections of the immediate past,* especially from the intellectual legacy left by Pius XII. In the history of the Church, the "old" and the "new" are always closely interwoven. The "new" grows out of the "old", and the "old" finds a fuller expression in the "new". Thus it was for the Second Vatican Council and for the activity of the Popes connected with the Council, starting with John XXIII, continuing with Paul VI and John Paul I, up to the present Pope.

What these Popes have accomplished during and since the Council, in their Magisterium no less than in their pastoral activity, has certainly made a significant contribution to the *preparation of that new springtime of Christian life* which will be revealed by the Great Jubilee, if Christians are docile to the action of the Holy Spirit.

19.   The Council, while not imitating the sternness of John the Baptist who called for repentance and conversion on the banks of the Jordan (cf. *Lk* 3:1-7), did show something of the Prophet of old, pointing out with fresh vigour to the men and women of today that Jesus Christ is the

"Lamb of God who takes away the sin of the world" (*Jn* 1:29), the Redeemer of humanity and the Lord of history. During the Council, precisely out of a desire to be fully faithful to her Master, the Church questioned herself about her own identity, and discovered anew the depth of her mystery as the Body and the Bride of Christ. Humbly heeding the word of God, she reaffirmed the universal call to holiness; she made provision for the reform of the liturgy, the "origin and summit" of her life; she gave impetus to the renewal of many aspects of her life at the universal level and in the local Churches; she strove to promote the various Christian vocations, from those of the laity to those of Religious, from the ministry of deacons to that of priests and Bishops; and in a particular way she rediscovered episcopal collegiality, that privileged expression of the pastoral service carried out by the Bishops in communion with the Successor of Peter. On the basis of this profound renewal, the Council opened itself to Christians of other denominations, to the followers of other religions and to all the people of our time. No Council had ever spoken so clearly about Christian unity, about dialogue with non-Christian religions, about the specific meaning of the Old Covenant and of Israel, about the dignity of each person's conscience, about the principle of religious liberty, about the different cultural traditions within which the Church carries out her missionary mandate, and about the means of social communication.

20.   The Council's enormously rich body of teaching and *the striking new tone* in the way it presented this content constitute as it were a proclamation of new times. The Council Fathers spoke in the language of the Gospel, the language of the Sermon on the Mount and the Beatitudes. In the Council's message God is presented *in his absolute lordship over all things,* but also as *the One who ensures the authentic autonomy of earthly realities.*

The best preparation for the new millennium, therefore, can only be expressed in a renewed commitment *to apply,* as faithfully as possible, *the teachings of Vatican II to the life of every individual and of the whole Church.* It was with the Second Vatican Council that, in the broadest sense of the term, the immediate preparations for the Great Jubilee of the Year 2000 were really begun. If we look for an analogy in the liturgy, it could be said that the yearly *Advent liturgy* is the season nearest to the spirit of the Council. For Advent prepares us to meet the One who was, who is and who is to come (cf. *Rev* 4:8).

21.   Part of the preparation for the approach of the Year 2000 is the *series of Synods* begun after the Second Vatican Council: general Synods together with continental, regional, national and diocesan Synods. The theme underlying them all is *evangelization,* or rather the new evangelization, the foundations of which were laid down in the Apostolic Exhortation *Evangelii Nuntiandi* of Pope Paul VI, issued in 1975 following the Third General As-

sembly of the Synod of Bishops. These Synods themselves are part of the new evangelization: they were born of the Second Vatican Council's vision of the Church. They open up broad areas for the participation of the laity, whose specific responsibilities in the Church they define. They are an expression of the strength which Christ has given to the entire People of God, making it a sharer in his own Messianic mission as Prophet, Priest and King. Very eloquent in this regard are the statements of the Dogmatic Constitution *Lumen Gentium. The preparation for the Jubilee Year 2000 is thus taking place throughout the whole Church, on the universal and local levels,* giving her a new awareness of the salvific mission she has received from Christ. This awareness is particularly evident in the Post-Synodal Exhortations devoted to the mission of the laity, the formation of priests, catechesis, the family, the value of penance and reconciliation in the life of the Church and of humanity in general, as well as in the forthcoming one to be devoted to the consecrated life.

22. Special tasks and responsibilities with regard to the Great Jubilee of the Year 2000 belong to the *ministry of the Bishop of Rome.* In a certain sense, all the Popes of the past century have prepared for this Jubilee. With his programme to renew all things in Christ, Saint Pius X tried to forestall the tragic developments which arose from the international situation at the beginning of this century. The Church was aware of her duty to act decisively to promote and defend the basic values

of peace and justice in the face of contrary tendencies in our time. The Popes of the period before the Council acted with firm commitment, each in his own way: Benedict XV found himself faced with the tragedy of the First World War; Pius XI had to contend with the threats of totalitarian systems or systems which did not respect human freedom in Germany, in Russia, in Italy, in Spain, and even earlier still in Mexico. Pius XII took steps to counter the very grave injustice brought about by a total contempt for human dignity at the time of the Second World War. He also provided enlightened guidelines for the birth of a new world order after the fall of the previous political systems.

Furthermore, in the course of this century the Popes, following in the footsteps of Leo XIII, systematically developed the themes of Catholic social doctrine, expounding the characteristics of a *just system* in the area of relations between labour and capital. We may recall the Encyclical *Quadragesimo Anno* of Pius XI, the numerous interventions of Pius XII, the Encyclicals *Mater et Magistra* and *Pacem in Terris* of John XXIII, the Encyclical *Populorum Progressio* and the Apostolic Letter *Octogesima Adveniens* of Paul VI. I too have frequently dealt with this subject: I specifically devoted the Encyclical *Laborem Exercens* to the importance of human labour, while in *Centesimus Annus* I wished to reaffirm the relevance, one hundred years later, of the doctrine presented in *Rerum Novarum*. In my Encyclical *Sollicitudo Rei Socialis* I had earlier offered a systematic refor-

30

mulation of the Church's entire social doctrine against the background of the East-West confrontation and the danger of nuclear war. The two elements of the Church's social doctrine—the *safeguarding of human dignity and rights* in the sphere of a just relation between labour and capital and *the promotion of peace*—were closely joined in this text. The Papal Messages of 1 January each year, begun in 1968 in the pontificate of Paul VI, are also meant to serve the cause of peace.

23.   Since the publication of the very first document of my Pontificate, *I have spoken explicitly of the Great Jubilee,* suggesting that the time leading up to it be lived as "a new Advent".[9] This theme has since reappeared many times, and was dwelt upon at length in the Encyclical *Dominum et Vivificantem.*[10] In fact, preparing for the *Year 2000 has become as it were a hermeneutical key of my Pontificate.* It is certainly not a matter of indulging in a new millenarianism, as occurred in some quarters at the end of the first millennium; rather, it is *aimed at an increased sensitivity to all that the Spirit is saying to the Church and to the Churches* (cf. *Rev* 2:7 ff.), as well as to individuals through charisms meant to serve the whole community. The purpose is to emphasize what the Spirit is suggesting to the different communities, from the smallest

[9] Encyclical Letter *Redemptor Hominis* (4 March 1979), 1: *AAS* 71 (1979), 258.
[10] Cf. Encyclical Letter *Dominum et Vivificantem* (18 May 1986), 49ff.: *AAS* 78 (1986), 868ff.

ones, such as the family, to the largest ones, such as nations and international organizations, taking into account cultures, societies and sound traditions. Despite appearances, humanity continues to await the revelation of the children of God, and lives by this hope, like a mother in labour, to use the image employed so powerfully by Saint Paul in his Letter to the Romans (cf. 8:19-22).

24. *Papal Journeys* have become an important element in the work of implementing the Second Vatican Council. Begun by John XXIII on the eve of the Council with a memorable pilgrimage to Loreto and Assisi (1962), they notably increased under Paul VI who, after first visiting the Holy Land (1964), undertook nine other great apostolic journeys which brought him into direct contact with the peoples of the different continents.

The current Pontificate has widened this programme of travels even further, starting with Mexico, on the occasion of the Third General Conference of the Latin American Episcopate held in Puebla in 1979. In that same year, there was also the trip to Poland for the Jubilee of the nine hundredth anniversary of the death of Saint Stanislaus, Bishop and Martyr.

The successive stages of these travels are well known. Papal journeys have become a regular occurrence, taking in the particular Churches in every continent and showing concern *for the development of ecumenical relationships* with Christians of various denominations. Particularly important in this regard were the visits to Turkey (1979),

Germany (1980), England, Scotland and Wales (1982), Switzerland (1984), the Scandinavian countries (1989), and most recently the Baltic countries (1993).

At present, it is my fervent wish to visit Sarajevo in Bosnia-Hercegovina and the Middle East: Lebanon, Jerusalem and the Holy Land. It would be very significant if in the Year 2000 it were possible to visit the *places on the road taken by the People of God of the Old Covenant,* starting from the places associated with Abraham and Moses, through Egypt and Mount Sinai, as far as Damascus, the city which witnessed the conversion of Saint Paul.

25.   In preparing for the Year 2000, *the individual Churches* have their own role to play, as they celebrate with their own Jubilees significant stages in the salvation history of the various peoples. Among these regional or *local Jubilees,* events of great importance have included the millennium of the Baptism of Rus' in 1988 [11] as also the five hundredth anniversary of the beginning of evangelization in America (1492). Besides events of such wide-ranging impact, we may recall others which, although not of universal importance, are no less significant: for example, the millennium of the Baptism of Poland in 1966 and of the Baptism of Hungary in 1968, together with the six hundredth anniversary of the Baptism of Lithua-

[11] Cf. Apostolic Letter *Euntes in Mundum* (25 January 1988): *AAS* 80 (1988), 935-956.

nia in 1987. There will soon also be celebrated the 1500th anniversary of the Baptism of Clovis (496), king of the Franks, and the 1400th anniversary of the arrival of Saint Augustine in Canterbury (597), marking the beginning of the evangelization of the Anglo-Saxon world.

As far as Asia is concerned, the Jubilee will remind us of the Apostle Thomas, who, according to tradition, brought the proclamation of the Gospel at the very beginning of the Christian era to India, where missionaries from Portugal would not arrive until about the year 1500. The current year also marks the seventh centenary of the evangelization of China (1294), and we are preparing to commemorate the spread of missionary work in the Philippines with the erection of the Metropolitan See of Manila (1595). We likewise look forward to the fourth centenary of the first martyrs in Japan (1597).

In Africa, where the first proclamation of the Gospel also dates back to Apostolic times, together with the 1650th anniversary of the episcopal consecration of the first Bishop of the Ethiopians, Saint Frumentius (c. 340), and the five hundredth anniversary of the beginning of the evangelization of Angola in the ancient Kingdom of the Congo (1491), nations such as Cameroon, Côte d'Ivoire, the Central African Republic, Burundi and Burkina Faso are celebrating the centenaries of the arrival of the first missionaries in their respective territories. Other African nations have recently celebrated such centenaries.

34

And how can we fail to mention the Eastern Churches, whose ancient Patriarchates are so closely linked to the apostolic heritage and whose venerable theological, liturgical and spiritual traditions constitute a tremendous wealth which is the common patrimony of the whole of Christianity? The many jubilee celebrations in these Churches, and in the Communities which acknowledge them as the origin of their own apostolicity, recall the journey of Christ down the centuries, leading to the Great Jubilee at the end of the second millennium.

Seen in this light, the whole of Christian history appears to us as a single river, into which many tributaries pour their waters. The Year 2000 invites us to gather with renewed fidelity and ever deeper communion *along the banks of this great river:* the river of Revelation, of Christianity and of the Church, a river which flows through human history starting from the event which took place at Nazareth and then at Bethlehem two thousand years ago. This is truly the "river" which with its "streams", in the expression of the Psalm, "make glad the city of God" (46:4).

26.   The *Holy Years* celebrated in the latter part of this century have also prepared for the Year 2000. *The Holy Year* proclaimed by Paul VI in *1975* is still fresh in our memory. The celebration of *1983 as the Year of Redemption* followed along the same lines. *The Marian Year 1986/87* perhaps struck a more resounding chord; it was eagerly awaited and profoundly experienced in the in-

dividual local Churches, especially at the Marian Shrines around the world. The Encyclical *Redemptoris Mater,* issued on that occasion, drew attention to the Council's teaching on the presence of the Mother of God in the mystery of Christ and the Church: two thousand years ago the Son of God was made man by the power of the Holy Spirit and was born of the Immaculate Virgin Mary. *The Marian Year was as it were an anticipation of the Jubilee,* and contained much of what will find fuller expression in the Year 2000.

27.   It would be difficult not to recall that the Marian Year took place only shortly before *the events of 1989.* Those events remain surprising for their vastness and especially for the speed with which they occurred. The Eighties were years marked by a growing danger from the "Cold War". 1989 ushered in a peaceful resolution which took the form, as it were, of an "organic" development. In the light of this fact, we are led to recognize a truly prophetic significance in the Encyclical *Rerum Novarum:* everything that Pope Leo XIII wrote there about Communism was borne out by these events, as I emphasized in the Encyclical *Centesimus Annus.*[12] In the unfolding of those events one could already discern the invisible hand of Providence at work with maternal care: "Can a woman forget her infant ...?" (*Is* 49:15).

<hr />

[12] Cf. Encyclical Letter *Centesimus Annus* (1 May 1991), 12: *AAS* 83 (1991), 807-809.

After 1989 however there arose *new dangers and threats*. In the countries of the former Eastern bloc, after the fall of Communism, there appeared the serious threat of exaggerated nationalism, as is evident from events in the Balkans and other neighbouring areas. This obliges the European nations to make a serious *examination of conscience*, and to acknowledge faults and errors, both economic and political, resulting from imperialist policies carried out in the previous and present centuries vis-à-vis nations whose rights have been systematically violated.

28.   In the wake of the Marian Year, we are now observing *the Year of the Family*, a celebration which is closely connected with the mystery of the Incarnation and with the very history of humanity. Thus there is good cause to hope that the Year of the Family, inaugurated at Nazareth, will become, like the Marian Year, *another significant stage in preparation for the Great Jubilee*.

With this in view, I wrote a *Letter to Families*, the purpose of which was to restate the substance of the Church's teaching on the family, and to bring this teaching, so to speak, into every home. At the Second Vatican Council, the Church recognized her duty to promote the dignity of marriage and the family.[13] The Year of the Family is meant to help make the Council's teaching in this

[13] Cf. Pastoral Constitution on the Church in the Modern World *Gaudium et Spes*, 47-52.

regard a reality. *Each family, in some way, should be involved in the preparation for the Great Jubilee.* Was it not through a family, the family of Nazareth, that the Son of God chose to enter into human history?

IV

IMMEDIATE PREPARATION

29.   Against the background of this sweeping panorama a question arises: can we draw up *a specific programme* of initiatives for the *immediate preparation* of the Great Jubilee? In fact, what has been said above already includes some elements of such a programme.

A more detailed plan of specific events will call for widespread consultation, in order for it not to be artificial and difficult to implement in the particular Churches, which live in such different conditions. For this reason, I wished to consult the Presidents of the Episcopal Conferences and especially the Cardinals.

I am grateful to the members of the College of Cardinals who met in Extraordinary Consistory on 13-14 June 1994, considered numerous proposals and suggested helpful guidelines. I also thank my Brothers in the Episcopate who in various ways communicated valuable ideas, which I have kept carefully in mind while writing this Apostolic Letter.

30.   The first recommendation which clearly emerged from the consultation regards *the period of preparation*. Only a few years now separate us

from the Year 2000: it seemed fitting to divide this period into *two phases,* reserving the *strictly preparatory* phase for the last three years. It was thought that the accumulation of many activities over the course of a longer period of preparation would detract from its spiritual intensity.

It was therefore considered appropriate to approach the historic date with a *first phase,* which would make the faithful aware of general themes, and then to concentrate the direct and immediate preparation into a *second phase* consisting of a *three-year period* wholly directed to the celebration of the mystery of Christ the Saviour.

a) FIRST PHASE

31.   *The first phase* will therefore be of an *ante-preparatory* character; it is meant to revive in the Christian people an awareness of the value and meaning of the Jubilee of the Year 2000 *in human history.* As a commemoration of the Birth of Christ, the Jubilee is *deeply charged with Christological significance.*

In keeping with the unfolding of the Christian faith in word and Sacrament, it seems important, even in this special anniversary, to link the structure of *memorial* with that of *celebration,* not limiting commemoration of the event only to ideas but also making its saving significance present through the celebration of the Sacraments. The Jubilee celebration should confirm the Christians of today in their *faith* in God who has revealed himself in Christ, sustain their *hope* which reaches out in expectation of eternal life, and rekindle their *charity* in active service to their brothers and sisters.

During the first stage (1994 to 1996) the Holy See, through a special *Committee* established for this purpose, will suggest courses of reflection and action at the universal level. A similar commitment to promoting awareness will be carried out in a more detailed way by corresponding *Commissions in the local Churches*. In a way, it is a question of continuing what was done in the period of remote preparation and at the same time of *coming to a deeper appreciation of the most significant aspects of the Jubilee celebration*.

32.   A Jubilee is always an occasion of special grace, "a day blessed by the Lord". As has already been noted, it is thus a time of joy. The Jubilee of the Year 2000 is meant to be a great *prayer of praise and thanksgiving*, especially for the *gift of the Incarnation of the Son of God and of the Redemption* which he accomplished. In the Jubilee Year Christians will stand with the renewed wonder of faith before the love of the Father, who *gave his Son*, "that whoever believes in him should not perish but have eternal life" (*Jn* 3:16). With a profound sense of commitment, they will likewise express their gratitude for the *gift of the Church*, established by Christ as "a kind of sacrament or sign of intimate union with God, and of the unity of all mankind".[14] Their thanksgiving will embrace

[14] SECOND VATICAN ECUMENICAL COUNCIL, Dogmatic Constitution on the Church *Lumen Gentium*, 1.

the *fruits of holiness* which have matured in the life of all those many men and women who in every generation and every period of history have fully welcomed the gift of Redemption.

Nevertheless, the joy of every Jubilee is above all a *joy based upon the forgiveness of sins, the joy of conversion.* It therefore seems appropriate to emphasize once more the theme of the *Synod of Bishops in 1984: penance and reconciliation.*[15] That Synod was an event of extraordinary significance in the life of the post-conciliar Church. It took up the ever topical question of conversion (*"meta-noia"*), which is the pre-condition for reconciliation with God on the part of both individuals and communities.

33. Hence it is appropriate that, as the Second Millennium of Christianity draws to a close, the Church should become more fully conscious of the sinfulness of her children, recalling all those times in history when they departed from the spirit of Christ and his Gospel and, instead of offering to the world the witness of a life inspired by the values of faith, indulged in ways of thinking and acting which were truly *forms of counter-witness and scandal.*

Although she is holy because of her incorporation into Christ, the Church does not tire of doing penance: before God and man *she always acknowledges as her own her sinful sons and daughters.* As

[15] Cf. Apostolic Exhortation *Reconciliatio et Paenitentia* (2 December 1984): *AAS* 77 (1985), 185-275.

Lumen Gentium affirms: "The Church, embracing sinners to her bosom, is at the same time holy and always in need of being purified, and incessantly pursues the path of penance and renewal".[16]

The Holy Door of the Jubilee of the Year 2000 should be symbolically wider than those of previous Jubilees, because humanity, upon reaching this goal, will leave behind not just a century but a millennium. It is fitting that the Church should make this passage with a clear awareness of what has happened to her during the last ten centuries. She cannot cross the threshold of the new millennium without encouraging her children to purify themselves, through repentance, of past errors and instances of infidelity, inconsistency, and slowness to act. Acknowledging the weaknesses of the past is an act of honesty and courage which helps us to strengthen our faith, which alerts us to face today's temptations and challenges and prepares us to meet them.

34.   Among the sins which require a greater commitment to repentance and conversion should certainly be counted those which *have been detrimental to the unity willed by God for his People.* In the course of the thousand years now drawing to a close, even more than in the first millennium, ecclesial communion has been painfully wounded, a fact "for which, at times, men of both sides were

---

[16] SECOND VATICAN ECUMENICAL COUNCIL, Dogmatic Constitution on the Church *Lumen Gentium,* 8.

to blame".[17] Such wounds openly contradict the will of Christ and are a cause of scandal to the world.[18] These sins of the past unfortunately still burden us and remain ever present temptations. It is necessary to make amends for them, and earnestly to beseech Christ's forgiveness.

In these last years of the millennium, the Church should invoke the Holy Spirit with ever greater insistence, imploring from him the grace of *Christian unity*. This is a crucial matter for our testimony to the Gospel before the world. Especially since the Second Vatican Council many ecumenical initiatives have been undertaken with generosity and commitment: it can be said that the whole activity of the local Churches and of the Apostolic See has taken on an ecumenical dimension in recent years. The *Pontifical Council for the Promotion of Christian Unity* has become an important catalyst in the movement towards full unity.

We are all however aware that the attainment of this goal cannot be the fruit of human efforts alone, vital though they are. *Unity, after all, is a gift of the Holy Spirit.* We are asked to respond to this gift responsibly, without compromise in our witness to the truth, generously implementing the guidelines laid down by the Council and in subsequent documents of the Holy See, which are also highly regarded by many Christians not in full communion with the Catholic Church.

---

[17] SECOND VATICAN ECUMENICAL COUNCIL, Decree on Ecumenism *Unitatis Redintegratio, 3.*
[18] Cf. *ibid.,* 1.

This then is one of the tasks of Christians as we make our way to the Year 2000. The approaching end of the second millennium demands of everyone an *examination of conscience* and the promotion of fitting ecumenical initiatives, so that we can celebrate the Great Jubilee, if not completely united, *at least much closer to overcoming the divisions of the second millennium.* As everyone recognizes, an enormous effort is needed in this regard. It is essential not only to continue along the path of dialogue on doctrinal matters, but above all to be more committed to *prayer for Christian unity.* Such prayer has become much more intense after the Council, but it must increase still more, involving an ever greater number of Christians, in unison with the great petition of Christ before his Passion: "Father ... that they also may all be one in us" (*Jn* 17:21).

35. Another painful chapter of history to which the sons and daughters of the Church must return with a spirit of repentance is that of the acquiescence given, especially in certain centuries, to *intolerance and even the use of violence* in the service of truth.

It is true that an accurate historical judgment cannot prescind from careful study of the cultural conditioning of the times, as a result of which many people may have held in good faith that an authentic witness to the truth could include suppressing the opinions of others or at least paying no attention to them. Many factors frequently converged to create assumptions which justified intolerance and fostered an emotional climate from which only great spirits, truly free and filled with God, were in some way able to break free. Yet the consideration of mitigating factors does not exonerate the Church from the obligation to express profound regret for the weaknesses of so many of her sons and daughters who sullied her face, preventing her from fully mirroring the image of her crucified Lord, the supreme witness of patient love and of humble meekness. From these painful moments of the past a lesson can be drawn for the future, leading all Christians to adhere fully to the sublime principle stated by the Council: "The truth cannot impose itself except by virtue of its own truth, as it wins over the mind with both gentleness and power".[19]

36.   Many Cardinals and Bishops expressed the desire for a serious examination of conscience above all on the part of *the Church of today*. On the threshold of the new Millennium Christians need to place themselves humbly before the Lord and examine themselves on *the responsibility which they too have for the evils of our day*. The present age in fact, together with much light, also presents not a few shadows.

How can we remain silent, for example, about the *religious indifference* which causes many people today to live as if God did not exist, or to be content with a vague religiosity, incapable of coming

[19] SECOND VATICAN ECUMENICAL COUNCIL, Declaration on Religious Freedom *Dignitatis Humanae,* 1.

to grips with the question of truth and the requirement of consistency? To this must also be added the widespread loss of the transcendent sense of human life, and confusion in the ethical sphere, even about the fundamental values of respect for life and the family. The sons and daughters of the Church too need to examine themselves in this regard. To what extent have they been shaped by the climate of secularism and ethical relativism? And what responsibility do they bear, in view of the increasing lack of religion, for not having shown the true face of God, by having "failed in their religious, moral, or social life"? [20]

It cannot be denied that, for many Christians, the spiritual life is passing through *a time of uncertainty* which affects not only their moral life but also their life of prayer and the *theological correctness of their faith.* Faith, already put to the test by the challenges of our times, is sometimes disoriented by erroneous theological views, the spread of which is abetted by the crisis of obedience vis-à-vis the Church's Magisterium.

And with respect to the Church of our time, how can we not lament *the lack of discernment,* which at times became even acquiescence, shown by many Christians concerning the violation of fundamental human rights by totalitarian regimes? And should we not also regret, among the shadows of our own day, the responsibility shared by

[20] SECOND VATICAN ECUMENICAL COUNCIL, Pastoral Constitution on the Church in the Modern World *Gaudium et Spes,* 19.

so many Christians *for grave forms of injustice and exclusion?* It must be asked how many Christians really know and put into practice the principles of the Church's social doctrine.

An examination of conscience must also consider the *reception given to the Council,* this great gift of the Spirit to the Church at the end of the second millennium. To what extent has the word of God become more fully the soul of theology and the inspiration of the whole of Christian living, as *Dei Verbum* sought? Is the liturgy lived as the "origin and summit" of ecclesial life, in accordance with the teaching of *Sacrosanctum Concilium?* In the universal Church and in the particular Churches, is the ecclesiology of communion described in *Lumen Gentium* being strengthened? Does it leave room for charisms, ministries, and different forms of participation by the People of God, without adopting notions borrowed from democracy and sociology which do not reflect the Catholic vision of the Church and the authentic spirit of Vatican II? Another serious question is raised by the nature of relations between the Church and the world. The Council's guidelines—set forth in *Gaudium et Spes* and other documents—of open, respectful and cordial dialogue, yet accompanied by careful discernment and courageous witness to the truth, remain valid and call us to a greater commitment.

37.   The Church of the first millennium was born of the blood of the martyrs: *"Sanguis martyr-*

um - semen christianorum".[21] The historical events linked to the figure of Constantine the Great could never have ensured the development of the Church as it occurred during the first millennium if it had not been for the *seeds sown by the martyrs and the heritage of sanctity which marked the first Christian generations.* At the end of the second millennium, *the Church has once again become a Church of martyrs.* The persecutions of believers —priests, Religious and laity—has caused a great sowing of martyrdom in different parts of the world. The witness to Christ borne even to the shedding of blood has become a common inheritance of Catholics, Orthodox, Anglicans and Protestants, as Pope Paul VI pointed out in his Homily for the Canonization of the Ugandan Martyrs.[22]

This witness must not be forgotten. The Church of the first centuries, although facing considerable organizational difficulties, took care to write down in special martyrologies the witness of the martyrs. These martyrologies have been constantly updated through the centuries, and the register of the saints and the blessed bears the names not only of those who have shed their blood for Christ but also of teachers of the faith, missionaries, confessors, bishops, priests, virgins, married couples, widows and children.

In our own century the martyrs have returned, many of them nameless, *"unknown soldiers"* as it

---

[21] TERTULLIAN, *Apol.*, 50:13: *CCL* I:171.
[22] Cf. *AAS* 56 (1964), 906.

were *of God's great cause.* As far as possible, their witness should not be lost to the Church. As was recommended in the Consistory, *the local Churches should do everything possible to ensure that the memory of those who have suffered martyrdom should be safeguarded, gathering the necessary documentation.* This gesture cannot fail to have an ecumenical character and expression. Perhaps the most convincing form of ecumenism is *the ecumenism of the saints* and of the martyrs. The *communio sanctorum* speaks louder than the things which divide us. The *martyrologium* of the first centuries was the basis of the veneration of the Saints. By proclaiming and venerating the holiness of her sons and daughters, the Church gave supreme honour to God himself; in the martyrs she venerated Christ, who was at the origin of their martyrdom and of their holiness. In later times there developed the practice of canonization, a practice which still continues in the Catholic Church and in the Orthodox Churches. In recent years the number of canonizations and beatifications has increased. These show the *vitality of the local Churches,* which are much more numerous today than in the first centuries and in the first millennium. The greatest homage which all the Churches can give to Christ on the threshold of the third millennium will be to manifest the Redeemer's all-powerful presence through the fruits of faith, hope and charity present in men and women of many different tongues and races who have followed Christ in the various forms of the Christian vocation.

It will be the task of the Apostolic See, in preparation for the Year 2000, *to update the martyrologies* for the universal Church, paying careful attention to the holiness of those who *in our own time* lived fully by the truth of Christ. In particular, there is a need to foster the recognition of the heroic virtues of men and women who have lived their Christian vocation *in marriage*. Precisely because we are convinced of the abundant fruits of holiness in the married state, we need to find the most appropriate means for discerning them and proposing them to the whole Church as a model and encouragement for other Christian spouses.

38.   A further need emphasized by the Cardinals and Bishops is that of *Continental Synods,* following the example of those already held for Europe and Africa. The last General Conference of the Latin American Episcopate accepted, in agreement with the Bishops of North America, the proposal for *a Synod for the Americas* on the problems of the new evangelization in both parts of the same continent, so different in origin and history, and on issues of justice and of international economic relations, in view of the enormous gap between North and South.

Another plan for a continent-wide Synod will concern *Asia,* where the issue of the encounter of Christianity with ancient local cultures and religions is a pressing one. This is a great challenge for evangelization, since religious systems such as Buddhism or Hinduism have a clearly soteriological character. There is also an urgent need for a Synod on the occasion of the Great Jubilee in order to illustrate and explain more fully the truth that Christ is the one Mediator between God and man and the sole Redeemer of the world, to be clearly distinguished from the founders of other great religions. With sincere esteem, the Church regards the elements of truth found in those religions as a reflection of the Truth which enlightens all men and women.[23] *"Ecce natus est nobis Salvator mundi"*: in the Year 2000 the proclamation of this truth should resound with renewed power.

Also for *Oceania* a Regional Synod could be useful. In this region there arises the question, among others, of the Aboriginal People, who in a unique way evoke aspects of human prehistory. In this Synod a matter not to be overlooked, together with other problems of the region, would be the encounter of Christianity with the most ancient forms of religion, profoundly marked by a monotheistic orientation.

b) SECOND PHASE

39.   On the basis of this vast programme aimed at creating awareness, it will then be possible to begin the *second phase,* the strictly *preparatory* phase. This will take place *over the span of three years,* from 1997 to 1999. The thematic structure

---

[23] Cf. SECOND VATICAN ECUMENICAL COUNCIL, Declaration on the Relation of the Church to Non-Christian Religions *Nostra Aetate,* 2.

of this three-year period, *centred on Christ,* the Son of God made man, must necessarily be theological, and therefore *Trinitarian.*

Year One: Jesus Christ

40.   *The first year,* 1997, will thus be devoted to *reflection on Christ,* the Word of God, made man by the power of the Holy Spirit. *The distinctly Christological character of the Jubilee* needs to be emphasized, for it will celebrate the Incarnation and coming into the world of the Son of God, the mystery of salvation for all mankind. The general theme proposed by many Cardinals and Bishops for this year is: *"Jesus Christ, the one Saviour of the world, yesterday, today and for ever"* (cf. *Heb* 13:8).

Among the Christological themes suggested in the Consistory the following stand out: a renewed appreciation of Christ, Saviour and Proclaimer of the Gospel, with special reference to the fourth chapter of the Gospel of Luke, where the theme of Christ's mission of preaching the Good News and the theme of the Jubilee are interwoven; a deeper understanding of the mystery of the Incarnation and of Jesus' birth from the Virgin Mary; the necessity of faith in Christ for salvation. In order to recognize who Christ truly is, Christians, especially in the course of this year, *should turn with renewed interest to the Bible,* "whether it be through the liturgy, rich in the divine word, or through devotional reading, or through instructions suitable for the purpose and other aids".[24] In the revealed text it is the Heavenly Father himself who comes to us in love and who dwells with us, disclosing to us the nature of his only-begotten Son and his plan of salvation for humanity.[25]

41.   The commitment, mentioned earlier, to make the mystery of salvation sacramentally present can lead, in the course of the year, to a *renewed appreciation of Baptism* as the basis of Christian living, according to the words of the Apostle: "As many of you as were baptized into Christ have put on Christ" (*Gal* 3:27). The *Catechism of the Catholic Church,* for its part, recalls that Baptism constitutes "the foundation of communion among all Christians, including those who are not yet in full communion with the Catholic Church".[26] From an *ecumenical point of view,* this will certainly be a very important year for Christians to look together to Christ the one Lord, deepening our commitment to become one in him, in accordance with his prayer to the Father. This emphasis on the centrality of Christ, of the word of God and of faith ought to inspire interest among Christians of other denominations and meet with a favourable response from them.

---

[24] SECOND VATICAN ECUMENICAL COUNCIL, Dogmatic Constitution on Divine Revelation *Dei Verbum,* 25.
[25] Cf. *ibid.,* 2.
[26] *Catechism of the Catholic Church,* No. 1271.

54

42.   Everything ought to focus on the primary objective of the Jubilee: the *strengthening of faith and of the witness of Christians.* It is therefore necessary to inspire in all the faithful *a true longing for holiness,* a deep desire for conversion and personal renewal in a context of ever more intense prayer and of solidarity with one's neighbour, especially the most needy.

The first year therefore will be the opportune moment for a renewed appreciation of *catechesis* in its original meaning as "the Apostles' teaching" (*Acts* 2:42) about the person of Jesus Christ and his mystery of salvation. In this regard, a detailed study of the *Catechism of the Catholic Church* will prove of great benefit, for the Catechism presents "faithfully and systematically ... the teaching of Sacred Scripture, the living Tradition of the Church and the authentic Magisterium, as well as the spiritual heritage of the Fathers, Doctors and Saints of the Church, to allow for a better knowledge of the Christian mystery and for enlivening the faith of the People of God".[27] To be realistic, we need to enlighten the consciences of the faithful concerning errors regarding the person of Christ, clarifying objections against him and against the Church.

43.   *The Blessed Virgin* who will be as it were "indirectly" present in the whole preparatory phase, will be contemplated in this first year espe-

---

[27] Apostolic Constitution *Fidei Depositum* (11 October 1992).

cially in the mystery of her Divine Motherhood. It was in her womb that the Word became flesh! The affirmation of the central place of Christ cannot therefore be separated from the recognition of the role played by his Most Holy Mother. Veneration of her, when properly understood, can in no way take away from "the dignity and efficacy of Christ the one Mediator".[28] Mary in fact constantly points to her Divine Son and she is proposed to all believers as the *model of faith* which is put into practice. "Devotedly meditating on her and contemplating her in the light of the Word made man, the Church with reverence enters more intimately into the supreme mystery of the Incarnation and becomes ever increasingly like her Spouse".[29]

Year Two: the Holy Spirit

44.   1998, the *second year* of the preparatory phase, will be dedicated in a particular way to the *Holy Spirit* and to his sanctifying presence within the Community of Christ's disciples. "The *great Jubilee* at the close of the second Millennium ...", I wrote in the Encyclical *Dominum et Vivificantem,* "has a *pneumatological aspect,* since the mystery of the Incarnation was accomplished 'by the power of the Holy Spirit'. It was 'brought about' by that Spirit—consubstantial with the Father and the

---

[28] SECOND VATICAN ECUMENICAL COUNCIL, Dogmatic Constitution on the Church *Lumen Gentium,* 62.
[29] *Ibid.,* 65.

Son—who, in the absolute mystery of the Triune God, is the Person-love, the uncreated gift, who is the eternal source of every gift that comes from God in the order of creation, the direct principle and, in a certain sense, the subject of God's self-communication in the order of grace. The *mystery of the Incarnation constitutes the climax* of this giving, this divine self-communication".[30]

The Church cannot prepare for the new millennium "in any other way than *in the Holy Spirit. What was accomplished by the power of the Holy Spirit 'in the fullness of time' can only through the Spirit's power now emerge from the memory of the Church".[31]

The Spirit, in fact, makes present in the Church of every time and place the unique Revelation brought by Christ to humanity, making it alive and active in the soul of each individual: "The Counsellor, the Holy Spirit, whom the Father will send in my name, he will teach you all things, and bring to your remembrance all that I have said to you" (*Jn* 14:26).

45.   The primary tasks of the preparation for the Jubilee thus include *a renewed appreciation of the presence and activity of the Spirit,* who acts within the Church both in the Sacraments, especially in *Confirmation,* and in the variety of charisms, roles and ministries which he inspires for the good

[30] Encyclical Letter *Dominum et Vivificantem* (18 May 1986), 50: *AAS* 78 (1986), 869-870.
[31] *Ibid.,* 51: *AAS* 78 (1986), 871.

of the Church: "There is only one Spirit who, according to his own richness and the needs of the ministries, distributes his different gift for the welfare of the Church (cf. *1 Cor* 12:1-11). Among these gifts stands out the grace given to the Apostles. To their authority, the Spirit himself subjected even those who were endowed with charisms (cf. *1 Cor* 14). Giving the body unity through himself and through his power and through the internal cohesion of its members, this same Spirit produces and urges love among the believers".[32]

In our own day too, the Spirit is *the principal agent of the new evangelization.* Hence it will be important to gain a renewed appreciation of the Spirit as the One who builds the Kingdom of God within the course of history and prepares its full manifestation in Jesus Christ, stirring people's hearts and quickening in our world the seeds of the full salvation which will come at the end of time.

46.   In this *eschatological perspective,* believers should be called to a renewed appreciation of the theological virtue *of hope,* which they have already heard proclaimed "in the word of the truth, the Gospel" (*Col* 1:5). The basic attitude of hope, on the one hand encourages the Christian not to lose sight of the final goal which gives meaning and value to life, and on the other, offers solid and profound reasons for a daily commitment to trans-

---

[32] SECOND VATICAN ECUMENICAL COUNCIL, Dogmatic Constitution on the Church *Lumen Gentium,* 7.

form reality in order to make it correspond to God's plan.

As the Apostle Paul reminds us: "We know that the whole creation has been groaning in travail together until now; and not only the creation, but we ourselves, who have the first fruits of the Spirit, groan inwardly as we wait for adoption as sons, the redemption of our bodies. For in this hope we were saved" (*Rom* 8:22-24). Christians are called to prepare for the Great Jubilee of the beginning of the Third Millennium *by renewing their hope in the definitive coming of the Kingdom of God,* preparing for it daily in their hearts, in the Christian community to which they belong, in their particular social context, and in world history itself.

There is also need for a better appreciation and understanding of *the signs of hope present in the last part of this century,* even though they often remain hidden from our eyes. *In society in general,* such signs of hope include: scientific, technological and especially medical progress in the service of human life, a greater awareness of our responsibility for the environment, efforts to restore peace and justice wherever they have been violated, a desire for reconciliation and solidarity among different peoples, particularly in the complex relationship between the North and the South of the world. *In the Church,* they include a greater attention to the voice of the Spirit through the acceptance of charisms and the promotion of the laity, a deeper commitment to the cause of Christian unity and the increased interest in dialogue with other religions and with contemporary culture.

47. The reflection of the faithful in the second year of preparation ought to focus particularly *on the value of unity* within the Church, to which the various gifts and charisms bestowed upon her by the Spirit are directed. In this regard, it will be opportune to promote a deeper understanding of the ecclesiological doctrine of the Second Vatican Council as contained primarily in the Dogmatic Constitution *Lumen Gentium*. This important document has expressly emphasized that the unity of the Body of Christ *is founded on the activity of the Spirit,* guaranteed by the Apostolic Ministry and sustained by mutual love (cf. *1 Cor* 13:1-8). This catechetical enrichment of the faith cannot fail to bring the members of the People of God to a more mature awareness of their own responsibilities, as well as to a more lively sense of the importance of ecclesial obedience.[33]

48. *Mary,* who conceived the Incarnate Word by the power of the Holy Spirit and then in the whole of her life allowed herself to be guided by his interior activity, will be contemplated and imitated during this year above all as the woman who was docile to the voice of the Spirit, a woman of silence and attentiveness, a woman of hope who, like Abraham, accepted God's will "hoping

[33] Cf. *ibid.,* 37.

against hope" (cf. *Rom* 4:18). Mary gave full expression to the longing of the poor of Yahweh and is a radiant model for those who entrust themselves with all their hearts to the promises of God.

Year Three: God the Father

49.   1999, *the third and final year of preparation,* will be aimed at broadening the horizons of believers, so that they will see things in the perspective of Christ: *in the perspective of the "Father who is in heaven"* (cf. *Mt* 5:45), from whom the Lord was sent and to whom he has returned (cf. *Jn* 16:28).

"This is eternal life, that they know you the only true God, and Jesus Christ whom you have sent" (*Jn* 17:3). The whole of the Christian life is like a great *pilgrimage to the house of the Father,* whose unconditional love for every human creature, and in particular for the "prodigal son" (cf. *Lk* 15:11-32), we discover anew each day. This pilgrimage takes place in the heart of each person, extends to the believing community and then reaches to the whole of humanity.

The Jubilee, centred on the person of Christ, thus becomes a great act of praise to the Father: "Blessed be the God and Father of our Lord Jesus Christ, who has blessed us in Christ with every spiritual blessing in the heavenly places, even as he chose us in him before the foundation of the world, that we should be holy and blameless before him" (*Eph* 1:3-4).

50.   In this third year the sense of being on a "journey to the Father" should encourage everyone to undertake, by holding fast to Christ the Redeemer of man, a journey of authentic *conversion*. This includes both a "negative" aspect, that of liberation from sin, and a "positive" aspect, that of choosing good, accepting the ethical values expressed in the natural law, which is confirmed and deepened by the Gospel. This is the proper context for a renewed appreciation and more intense celebration of the *Sacrament of Penance* in its most profound meaning. The call to conversion as the indispensable condition of Christian love is particularly important in contemporary society, where the very foundations of an ethically correct vision of human existence often seem to have been lost.

It will therefore be necessary, especially during this year, to emphasize the theological virtue of *charity*, recalling the significant and lapidary words of the First Letter of John: "God is love" (4:8,16). Charity, in its twofold reality as love of God and neighbour is the summing up of the moral life of the believer. It has in God its source and its goal.

51.   From this point of view, if we recall that Jesus came to "preach the good news to the poor" (*Mt* 11:5; *Lk* 7:22), how can we fail to lay greater emphasis on the *Church's preferential option for the poor and the outcast?* Indeed, it has to be said that a commitment to justice and peace in a world like ours, marked by so many conflicts and intolerable

social and economic inequalities, is a necessary condition for the preparation and celebration of the Jubilee. Thus, in the spirit of the Book of Leviticus (25:8-12), Christians will have to raise their voice on behalf of all the poor of the world, proposing the Jubilee as an appropriate time to give thought, among other things, to reducing substantially, if not cancelling outright, the international debt which seriously threatens the future of many nations. The Jubilee can also offer an opportunity for reflecting on other challenges of our time, such as the difficulties of dialogue between different cultures and the problems connected with respect for women's rights and the promotion of the family and marriage.

52.   Recalling that "Christ ... by the revelation of the mystery of the Father and his love, fully reveals man to man himself and makes his supreme calling clear",[34] two commitments should characterize in a special way the third preparatory year: *meeting the challenge of secularism and dialogue with the great religions.*

With regard to the former, it will be fitting to broach the vast subject of the *crisis of civilization,* which has become apparent especially in the West, which is highly developed from the standpoint of technology but is interiorly impoverished by its tendency to forget God or to keep him at a distance. This crisis of civilization must be coun-

---

[34] SECOND VATICAN ECUMENICAL COUNCIL, Pastoral Constitution on the Church in the Modern World *Gaudium et Spes,* 22.

tered by *the civilization of love,* founded on the universal values of peace, solidarity, justice and liberty, which find their full attainment in Christ.

53.   On the other hand, as far as the field of religious awareness is concerned, the eve of the Year 2000 will provide a great opportunity, especially in view of the events of recent decades, for *interreligious dialogue,* in accordance with the specific guidelines set down by the Second Vatican Council in its Declaration *Nostra Aetate* on the relationship of the Church to non-Christian religions.

In this dialogue the Jews and the Muslims ought to have a pre-eminent place. God grant that as a confirmation of these intentions it may also be possible to hold *joint meetings* in places of significance for the great monotheistic religions.

In this regard, attention is being given to finding ways of arranging historic meetings in places of exceptional symbolic importance like Bethlehem, Jerusalem and Mount Sinai as a means of furthering dialogue with Jews and the followers of Islam, and to arranging similar meetings elsewhere with the leaders of the great world religions. However, care will always have be taken not to cause harmful misunderstandings, avoiding the risk of syncretism and of a facile and deceptive irenicism.

54.   In this broad perspective of commitments, *Mary Most Holy,* the highly favoured daughter of the Father, will appear before the eyes of believers as the perfect model of love towards both God and neighbour. As she herself says in the Canticle

of the *Magnificat,* great things were done for her by the Almighty, whose name is holy (cf. *Lk* 1:49). The Father chose her for a *unique mission* in the history of salvation: that of being the Mother of the long-awaited Saviour. The Virgin Mary responded to God's call with complete openness: "Behold, I am the handmaid of the Lord" (*Lk* 1:38). Her motherhood, which began in Nazareth and was lived most intensely in Jerusalem at the foot of the Cross, will be felt during this year as a loving and urgent invitation addressed to all the children of God, so that they will return to the house of the Father when they hear her maternal voice: "Do whatever Christ tells you" (cf. *Jn* 2:5).

c) APPROACHING THE CELEBRATION

55.   A separate chapter will be the *actual celebration of the Great Jubilee,* which will take place simultaneously in the Holy Land, in Rome and in the local Churches throughout the world. Especially in this phase, the *phase of celebration,* the aim will be *to give glory to the Trinity,* from whom everything in the world and in history comes and to whom everything returns. This mystery is the focus of the three years of immediate preparation: from Christ and through Christ, in the Holy Spirit, to the Father. In this sense the Jubilee celebration makes present in an anticipatory way the goal and fulfilment of the life of each Christian and of the whole Church in the Triune God.

But since Christ is the only way to the Father, in order to highlight his living and saving presence in the Church and the world, *the International Eucharistic Congress* will take place in Rome, on the occasion of the Great Jubilee. The Year 2000 will be intensely Eucharistic: in the *Sacrament of the Eucharist* the Saviour, who took flesh in Mary's womb twenty centuries ago, continues to offer himself to humanity as the source of divine life.

The ecumenical and universal character of the Sacred Jubilee can be fittingly reflected by a *meeting of all Christians*. This would be an event of great significance, and so, in order to avoid misunderstandings, it should be properly presented and carefully prepared, in an attitude of fraternal cooperation with Christians of other denominations and traditions, as well as of grateful openness to those religions whose representatives might wish to acknowledge the joy shared by all the disciples of Christ.

One thing is certain: everyone is asked to do as much as possible to ensure that the great challenge of the Year 2000 is not overlooked, for this challenge certainly involves a special grace of the Lord for the Church and for the whole of humanity.

V

"JESUS CHRIST
IS THE SAME ... FOR EVER"
(*Heb* 13:8)

56.   The Church has endured for 2000 years.
Like the *mustard seed* in the Gospel, she has
grown and become a great tree, able to cover the
whole of humanity with her branches (cf. *Mt*
13:31-32). The Second Vatican Council, in its
Dogmatic Constitution on the Church, thus ad-
dresses the question of *membership in the Church*
and the call of all people to belong to the People of
God: "All are called to be part of this Catholic
unity of the new People of God ... And there belong to it or are related to it in various ways, the
Catholic faithful as well as all who believe in
Christ, and indeed the whole of mankind, which
by the grace of God is called to salvation".[35] Pope
Paul VI, in the Encyclical *Ecclesiam Suam* illus-
trates how all mankind is involved in the plan of
God, and emphasizes the various *circles of the dia-*
logue of salvation.[36]

---

[35] SECOND VATICAN ECUMENICAL COUNCIL, Dogmatic Constitution on the Church *Lumen Gentium,* 13.

[36] Cf. PAUL VI, Encyclical Letter *Ecclesiam Suam* (6 August 1964),
III: *AAS* 56 (1964), 650-657.

Continuing this approach, we can also appreciate more clearly the Gospel parable of the leaven (cf. *Mt* 13:33): Christ, like a divine leaven, always and ever more fully penetrates the life of humanity, spreading the work of salvation accomplished in the Paschal Mystery. What is more, he embraces within his redemptive power *the whole past history* of the human race, beginning with the first Adam.[37] The *future* also belongs to him: "Jesus Christ is the same yesterday and today and for ever" (*Heb* 13:8). For her part the Church "seeks but a solitary goal: to carry forward the work of Christ himself under the lead of the Holy Spirit, the Paraclete. And Christ entered this world to give witness to the truth, to rescue and not to sit in judgment, to serve and not to be served".[38]

57.   Therefore, ever since the apostolic age, *the Church's mission* has continued without interruption within the whole human family. The first evangelization took place above all in the region of the Mediterranean. In the course of the first millennium, missions setting out from Rome and Constantinople brought Christianity to *the whole continent of Europe*. At the same time they made their way to the heart of *Asia,* as far as India and China. The end of the fifteenth century marked both the discovery of *America* and the beginning of the evangelization of that great continent,

---

[37] Cf. *ibid.,* 2.
[38] SECOND VATICAN ECUMENICAL COUNCIL, Pastoral Constitution on the Church in the Modern World *Gaudium et Spes,* 3.

North and South. Simultaneously, while the sub-Saharan coasts of Africa welcomed the light of Christ, Saint Francis Xavier, Patron of the Missions, reached Japan. At the end of the eighteenth century and the beginning of the nineteenth, a layman, Andrew Kim, brought Christianity to Korea. In the same period the proclamation of the Gospel reached Indochina, as well as *Australia and the Islands of the Pacific.*

The nineteenth century witnessed vast missionary activity among the *peoples of Africa.* All these efforts bore fruit which has lasted up to the present day. The Second Vatican Council gives an account of this in the Decree *Ad Gentes* on Missionary Activity. After the Council the question of missionary work was dealt with in the Encyclical *Redemptoris Missio,* in the light of the problems of the missions in these final years of our century. In the future too, the Church must continue to be missionary: indeed missionary outreach is part of her very nature. With the fall of the great anti-Christian systems in Europe, first of Nazism and then of Communism, there is urgent need to bring once more the liberating message of the Gospel to the men and women of Europe.[39] Furthermore, as the Encyclical *Redemptoris Missio* affirms, the modern world reflects the situation of the *Areopagus of Athens,* where Saint Paul spoke[40]. Today there are many "areopagi", and

[39] Cf. *Declaration* of the Special Assembly for Europe of the Synod of Bishops, No. 3.
[40] Cf. Encyclical Letter *Redemptoris Missio* (7 December 1990), 37: *AAS* 83 (1991), 284-286.

very different ones: these are the vast sectors of contemporary civilization and culture, of politics and economics. *The more the West is becoming estranged from its Christian roots, the more it is becoming missionary territory,* taking the form of many different "areopagi".

58.   The future of the world and the Church belongs to the *younger generation,* to those who, born in this century, will reach maturity in the next, the first century of the new millennium. *Christ expects great things from young people,* as he did from the young man who asked him: "What good deed must I do, to have eternal life?" (*Mt* 19:16). I have referred to the remarkable answer which Jesus gave to him, in the recent Encyclical *Veritatis Splendor,* as I did earlier, in 1985, in my *Apostolic Letter to the Youth of the World.* Young people, in every situation, in every region of the world, do not cease to put questions to Christ: *they meet him and they keep searching for him in order to question him further.* If they succeed in following the road which he points out to them, they will have the joy of making their own contribution to his presence in the next century and in the centuries to come, until the end of time: "Jesus is the same yesterday, today and for ever".

59.   In conclusion, it is helpful to recall the words of the Pastoral Constitution *Gaudium et Spes:* "The Church believes that Christ, who died and was raised up for all, can through his Spirit offer man the light and the strength to measure up

70

to his supreme destiny. Nor has any other name under heaven been given to man by which it is fitting for him to be saved. She likewise holds that *in her most benign Lord and Master can be found the key, the focal point, and the goal of all human history.* The Church also maintains that beneath all changes there are *so many realities which do not change and which have their ultimate foundation in Christ,* who is the same yesterday and today and for ever. Hence in the light of Christ, the image of the unseen God, the firstborn of every creature, the Council wishes to speak to all men in order to illuminate the mystery of man and to cooperate in finding the solution to the outstanding problems of our time".[41]

While I invite the faithful to raise to the Lord fervent prayers to obtain the light and assistance necessary for the preparation and celebration of the forthcoming Jubilee, I exhort my Venerable Brothers in the Episcopate and the ecclesial communities entrusted to them to open their hearts to the promptings of the Spirit. He will not fail to arouse enthusiasm and lead people to celebrate the Jubilee with renewed faith and generous participation.

I entrust this responsibility of the whole Church to the maternal intercession of Mary, Mother of the Redeemer. She, the Mother of Fairest Love, will be for Christians on the way to the Great Jubilee of the Third Millennium the Star

---

[41] Second Vatican Ecumenical Council, Pastoral Constitution on the Church in the Modern World *Gaudium et Spes*, 10.

71

which safely guides their steps to the Lord. May the unassuming Young Woman of Nazareth, who two thousand years ago offered to the world the Incarnate Word, lead the men and women of the new millennium towards the One who is "the true light that enlightens every man" (*Jn* 1:9).

With these sentiments I impart to all my Blessing.

From the Vatican, on 10 November in the year 1994, the seventeenth of my Pontificate.

Joannes Paulus PP. II